How To
Waking Up

A Hands-On Guide to Becoming a Morning Person

Sam Uyama

www.samuyama.com

"A great book to get your body and mind prepared for a new life"

"I loved this book"

"Exactly what it says on the tin"

"This book is packed with useful, hands on information"

"An excellent quick read with very practical tips & resources"

To Sun Myung Moon, the master at waking up early

Table of Contents

Introduction

Richard Branson, Founder of Virgin Group

Napoleon, French Conqueror

Howard Schultz, CEO of Starbucks

Dalai Lama, Religious Leader

Michelle Obama, First Lady of the United States

These are just a few of the many, many successful people who point their accomplishments to them being early risers. But how the heck do they do it? A quick Google search will turn up hundreds of articles on the benefits of waking up early and some tips on how to get out of bed. Some of them are helpful, but many repeat the same things. They'll say things like, "find something to be excited about in the morning", which is inspiring and somewhat helpful, but only works until it doesn't. One day the motivation is zapped and you go back to what you always did. Ultimately, there has yet to be a systematic approach on how to become a morning person.

If you're reading this book, it means something has drawn you to the early hours of the morning. For some it may be about having time to enjoy a favorite hobby. For others it may be about being more productive. Still others may want to get healthier. No matter the reason, this book will help you get there.

What qualifies me to write this book?

Many people have an earnest desire to wake up earlier but simply don't know how to manage it. They invest their time reading through blogs but nothing can provide what they're looking for. I want to offer something that will actually get you there, one man's journey to becoming an early riser. I know what it's like not being able to get up in the morning. I've had days where I tried and failed to get up early (a lot of them), and I've had days where I hated getting out of bed so much I made myself late for work. Some people have never had that problem. They've never had a hard time getting up whenever they want and their friends don't know how they do it. I was never one of those people. I've made the extra effort to go to bed extremely early and still not want to get up in the morning.

In college I became obsessed with the idea of mastering "waking up." I spent the better part of two years self-disciplining myself to get up at 5:00am or 6:00am (in college!), continuously struggling along the way. Not to mention how I would overindulge on weekends (much like people who diet are with food). But then something inside of me shifted, and getting up early was no longer a battle to be waged each morning. It became something that happened naturally. This change intrigued those who know me and I got enough questions to inspire me to write this book. My goal is to teach others how to make the shift from struggling to get up in the morning to waking up early being natural.

What this book is not:

Frankly, the easy answer to waking up early is going to bed earlier. But that's not news and definitely not worth buying a book about. It's also not enough to make a difference for most people. One of the most doctor-recommended New Year's Resolutions for Americans is to get more sleep*. People have been hearing they need to go to bed earlier for years, but somehow aren't able to manage it. And for those that do figure it out, getting up in the early hours is still a struggle, even with enough sleep.

This book is not a list of things that would be nice to do in the morning. It's not something I read somewhere and copied into a book. It's not a fly-by list of tips like "think positive" or "get at least 8 hours of sleep." There are plenty of blogs out there with great lists of things to do in the morning or how you can drag yourself out of bed.

*UMD Baltimore Washington Medical Center

What this book is:

This is the approach I used to learn to absolutely *love* waking up early in the morning. An early rise has become something I've come to love and can't imagine living without. That's what I want to provide for you.

Who this book is for:

This book is for those who want to fall in love with getting up early and being able to have time to do things that are important to them. It's for those that want to make early mornings a natural part of their daily life, but have struggled with it for as long as they can remember. And lastly, this book is for those who are willing to make a few lifestyle adjustments in order to make those desires a reality. This is about being easy and sustainable, but it's not a free ride.

What you get with this book:

The promise of this book is that you walk away with a clear method for how to get out of bed with ease and love being up early in the morning.

To fulfill on that promise what you'll get is a guide outlining exactly how I went from pulling myself out of bed like many people to waking up early being my favorite part of the day. This includes links to useful videos and blog posts, apps I found useful, and organizational tools I created to help me along the way.

What's important is what works for you, I'll make them all available and you can pick and choose what you like.

Note: *while this book is targeted specifically for people wanting to enjoy waking up early in the morning, much of what we'll cover works for people who struggle getting out of bed no matter the time.*

Chapter One: Setting the Stage

A quick look on Google will show that people who wake up early are more:

- Productive

- Healthy

- Optimistic

- Creative

Those are some of the benefits of waking up earlier, but what's the real juice to creating a lifestyle around being an early riser? Why would it be something I'm so passionate about? Not only does it allow you time for things you often neglect, but waking up before you "need" to get up is representative of taking control of your life. Be in school by 8:30. Be at work by 9:00. These are times that completely dictate how we live our lives, down to determining when we decide to wake up every morning. Choosing to go the extra mile is taking a stand. It says, "I'm in charge." It's a small step that has a huge impact on your sense of self-direction and satisfaction in life.

I wanted waking up early to become a natural part of my life, not a dramatic struggle every time the alarm went off. I couldn't find anything that offered that, so devised my own system. After research and experimentation this is the method I found that works.

Chapter Two: The Habit Loop

The first thing to explore is why getting up is so hard to begin with. It's somewhat of a running joke, you can read hundreds of blogs on people's struggles in the morning; we've created an entire culture around the morning coffee routine.

garfield.com

Note: *There are a lot of medical explanations for why people have a hard time getting up. Most of them can be checked with a simple blood test:*

- *Anemia (iron deficiency)*

- *Potassium Deficiency*

- *Under/Over Active Thyroid*

- *Diabetes*

Most things beyond those would require checking with a Sleep Lab. Sleep Apnea is another possibility, but unlikely if you don't already know you have it.

Any of these would carry their own challenges with waking up that we won't get into. This book is based on the assumption that you're capable of getting up if you really wanted to (airplane to catch, early start on a beach trip), you just have a really hard time with it.

The main problem with what I've found online is that nothing really addresses why it's such a struggle waking up early on the day to day. They offer suggestions, which I get excited to try for a few days, but then I just return to my normal pattern. When you really think about it, why *is it* so hard waking up in the morning?

The short answer is that it comes down to habits. Over the years I found I could get comfortably ready for the day in 45 minutes. This included washing up, eating a good breakfast, and getting together all the things I would need. I could get four hours of sleep and still get myself up for those 45 minutes.

Waking up any earlier than that is when it got hard. It wasn't part of my pattern. If I tried to wake up earlier, I'd get up to turn my alarm off and decide to lie back down for another 10 minutes. Next thing I know 2 hours have gone by and I have 45 minutes to get ready. I'd follow this pattern again and again, even knowing I'd fall asleep if I took that 10-minute nap.

During my research into habits I stumbled across a 16-minute YouTube clip* by Charles Duhigg, author of the best seller, "The Power of Habit." This video had a profound impact on me and became the cornerstone for how I learned to enjoy waking up.

In it, he discusses the neurological process of how our brains form habits. Our brains trigger actions in response to cues, with the expectation of some kind of reward. This reward then reinforces the action. That's how habits are formed. It made perfect sense why I was so engrained in my 45-minute routine and 10-minute nap trap. If I tried to wake up early my alarm going off was a cue I used to reward myself with a "10-minute" nap.

*You can find this video and all other links throughout this book at:

samuyama.com/love-waking-up

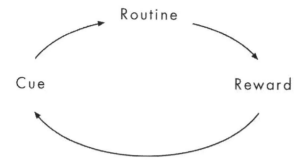

charlesduhigg.com

Most people likely have a default time they've conditioned themselves with that leaves them just enough time to get ready and be out of the house to wherever they need to go. If you needed to be out of the house by 8:00am in order to get somewhere, what time would you wake up? My guess is it would be the exact amount of time you needed to be ready by 8:00am. For some this would be 7:30am and other's 6:00am.

The main obstacle stopping us from waking up any earlier and actually enjoying it is this habit we've conditioned ourselves with. For most people there is no sense of reward attached to waking up any earlier (at least neurologically), and many people have actually conditioned themselves with habits that reward not getting up effectively (think snooze button).

I wanted time in the mornings so I could exercise, work on personal projects, and be able to plan for the day instead of rushing out of the house. My habit loop was what was stopping me from accomplishing those things. What excited me was realizing I could train my brain with a new habit loop and enjoy getting up earlier.

I decided to try a small habit for 30 days and see what happens. As soon as my alarm went off, no matter what time it was set for, I would pop a chocolate almond in my mouth. Some days I would still decide to go back to bed, but I made sure to eat my chocolate after turning off my alarm.

What I discovered from this experiment was getting out of bed became easier, my mood was better, and I was more likely to stay up instead of going back to sleep.

What clicked in my head was the idea that if I could make waking up measurably better with that little bit of work, could it be possible to develop a giant habit loop that lead to productive mornings?

Step 1:

Create a habit loop for immediately upon rising.

First, identify a **cue**, **action**, and **reward**. Here are the ones I came up with:

Cue: Alarm going off

Action: Turn off alarm

Reward: ~~Chocolate almond~~ COFFEE!

Find a reward that works for you. Gum, hard candy, some people just love brushing their teeth in the morning. Be creative.

Tips & Advice

- Take time on just this point and work towards making it a habit. Wait till you're confident with it before moving on to Step 2.

- Whatever habit loop you decide on, it's important that you treat this loop as sacred. For it to become effective it needs to become automatic, which takes repetition.

- I like to wake up using an app called "Sleep Cycle" by Northcube AB. It measures your activity while you sleep and calculates the best time to wake you within a timeframe. It can reveal interesting information on your sleeping habits, from what affects your sleep quality and at what hours you sleep best. What I really like is it has a 1-3 rating for how you feel when you wake up. This will let you track your progress to becoming a bonafide member of the Early Morning Club.

- In the beginning when I was still fixed on my 10-minute nap trap it was very effective to use two alarms. Sleep Cycle by my bed woke me 1-20 minutes before I planned on getting up, and another alarm across the room with my chocolate set for when I wanted to get out of bed.

Chapter Three: Bookending The Day

It's the end of the day. You're brushing your teeth thinking about how your day went and you're disappointed. There's a list of things you planned on doing but never got around to. You wanted to exercise, clean out your desk, and take some time to meditate. But then you got up late, got slammed with a last-minute deadline, and by the time you got home all you could manage was some food and TV before bed.

This story illustrates two more reasons why having time in the morning is a worthy endeavor:

- We never know what will pop up during the day, it's near impossible to adjust for the emergencies that come up and maintain a plan at the same time. The stuff we wanted to get done gets pushed back and we feel helpless.

- Willpower is a limited resource. Baumeister and his colleagues revealed this important discovery in the 2011 book, "Willpower." Not only that, but we use the same stock of willpower for every type of task. So the more things we deal with during the day the more it wears at our willpower. By the time we get home there's no way we're going to the gym, working on that vegetable garden, or any of the other things on our "one day, someday" list.

Thankfully there's a way to combat that. Step 1 will make a tremendous difference for your mornings, but next is to expand the habit loop and create a system of execution. This is a concept called "bookending your days." Aka, the Morning and Evening Routines.

I got this from Darren Hardy's book "The Compound Effect". It's naïve to think you can fully expect what will happen during the middle of the day - a myriad of things can throw you off your rhythm. What you can control are the ends, and luckily that's all you need.

The Morning Routine:

World-class results are built around world-class routines. If you ask high performers in any field (or examine areas of your life you excel in) you will find signs of a finely tuned routine. Athletes have their pre-game warm-ups, students have their favorite study spots, and pilots have their pre-flight checklists.

The purpose of our routine is to create an activity that habituates waking up and getting you ready for the day. It's something to guide you out of the waking up phase, get you in a positive state of mind, and prep you for a productive morning.

Step 2:

Create a 20-minute Morning Routine

Cue: Finish eating chocolate almond COFFEE!.

Action: Morning Routine

Reward: Check phone notifications

I chose 20-minutes because it's long enough to get a considerable task done and feel great about it, but short enough that it's sustainable and easy to transform into a habit. How you like to set up your routine is up to you, what's important is that it's concise and something you can do everyday.

You can use mine as a guideline:

- Wash face/put in contact lenses

- 2 minute stretch (just enough to loosen up)

- Handstand (something I've been working on & really wakes me up)

- 10 Deep Breathes

- Daily Planner*

*This planner is something I put together. It has everything I need to plan for the day and includes a few affirmations I use to get myself in a great state of mind. (Photo in "Tips & Advice" section")

Lastly, as a reward I check any notifications on my phone (I resist the urge to do so as soon as I wake up, so this is very satisfying for me).

That has me ready for the day. Despite whatever comes at me, I have clear objectives that act as a guidepost for how I go about my activities.

Tips & Advice

- Some people may be good with the help in waking up from Step 1 and want to get on with the rest of their morning. If so that's fine, but the morning routine played a crucial part in waking up early becoming a natural part of my life. It automated a few of the most important things I wanted to get done, adding to my fuel for the morning as opposed to being the first thing to wear at my willpower for the day.

- If I were to have time for only one thing in the morning it would be this planner. It's made that much of a difference for me. Here's a link with pdf/doc files for your use. Download* and print or edit it how you see fit. (Be kind to nature, print double-sided)

*Download at:

samuyama.com/love-waking-up

What can I do today that will make life truly worth living?

I realize that the dominating thoughts of my mind eventually reproduce themselves in outward bodily action and gradually transform themselves into physical reality. Therefore I will concentrate my mind upon the task of thinking of the person I intend to be and then transforming that picture into reality through practical service.

I fully realize that no wealth or position can long endure unless built with integrity. Therefore I will engage in no transaction that does not benefit all whom it affects. I will succeed by gaining the cooperation of other people. I will induce others to serve me, because I will first serve them. I will eliminate hatred, jealousy, selfishness, and cynicism by developing love for all humanity, because I know that a negative attitude towards others can never bring me success. I will cause others to believe in me, because I will believe in them and in myself.

And above all, I will accomplish my goals by rendering the highest quality service at the highest quantity I am capable, because action is the only thing that makes a difference.

MIT's	To Do's
"Most Important Tasks" for the day. Never more than three at a time.	

Morning	Evening
Stretch	Shower
Meditate	Stretch
Prep day	Complete Day
Exercise	Deep Breathes

Today I'm Grateful For......

- ●   ●
- ●   ●

2 Things I Will Send Love To

1)

2)

2 New Ideas

- ●   ●

Date:

5 am

6 am

7 am

8 am

9 am

10 am

11 am

12 pm

1 pm

2 pm

3 pm

4 pm

5 pm

6 pm

7 pm

8 pm

9 pm

Today I will live well. I will be generous with what I have to give. I will laugh deeply and smile often. I will not pursue a life of distraction and entertainment, but rather I will move intentionally forward in the purpose I have set for myself.

Signed: _____ x

- This will take more of you to accomplish than our first habit loop created in Step 1. It's okay to take it slow. Start with a set number of times a week you want to do your routine. Something like Monday-Friday or every other day works well.

- I'm always creating new productivity tools like the Daily Planner. If you'd like hear about new tools as well as be the first to hear about upcoming books you can email me at me@samuyama.com to be added to my mailing list.

The Evening Routine:

You can condition yourself all you want to enjoy waking up, but the reality is what makes the most difference is getting a good night's sleep. The Evening Routine is about winding down and brining closure to the day, getting relaxed and stopping everything going on in your life from running around your head. I've found this dramatically increases the quality of my sleep and is a great way to make sure I get to bed on time.

ep 3:

Create an Evening Routine

Cue: Alarm goes off at 9:00pm

Action: Evening Routine

Reward: Read a good book

Again, what's important is what works for you. The key components are that it's relaxing, long enough to fully detach you from the day's activities (I like 40 minutes), and involves some kind of preparation for the next day. I set an alarm for 9:00pm that acts as a cue to begin wrapping up the night.

Here's my Evening Routine:

- Shower and wash up.
- 10 min. stretch
- Prepare Daily Planner
- 15 deep breathes

After showering up I'll start the next day's Daily Planner. I don't spend long on it, I write down my schedule for the coming day and jot down my MITs (Most Important Tasks) and any to-dos I want to get done. This is key. It's my core system for keeping track of my goals, and allows me to relax and not worry about forgetting something because I know it's written down for me to work on in the morning.

After stretching and some deep breaths my day is complete. Sure, there are days that I don't get everything done that I wanted, but those 15 breaths mark my day as complete and what I didn't get to will be left for tomorrow.

I finish the night with 15-20 minutes of a good book before falling asleep.

Tips & Advice

- Use your Evening Routine to detach from all electronics as well. I put my phone on airplane mode before taking a shower.

- I like writing my To-Dos down on paper, but the reality is I'm not going to carry around my Daily Planner to keep track of what I want to do throughout the day. What works is I handwrite my MITs & to-dos the night before, and the next morning when filling out the rest of the Planner I go over them again and put them in a great app called "Wunderlist" by Six Wunderkinder. I like Wunderlist because it syncs between computer and smartphone, so I can keep track of what to do no matter where I'm working.

- There's a saying that goes "No one dies with an empty to-do list". Remember that life's not about finishing everything on your list because it's on your list. Your list is just a system to keep track of your tasks and goals. Don't expect to finish it all every single time and definitely don't let that stress you out.

Chapter Four: Completing Your Morning

Once you've got your Morning & Evening Routines down you'll be on track to love waking up each and every morning. That in itself will open up so many possibilities for your life. You'll be able to spend the early hours pursuing the things you felt you never had time for, not to mention how much your mood through the day will increase.

If you had a couple extra hours each morning what would you want to do with the time? That's a question worth asking yourself, and one only you can answer. You probably already had something in mind when you started this book, but here are a few things I'd suggest:

Something Healthy. 90% of people who exercise on a consistent basis do so in the morning*. Yoga, walking, gardening, whatever floats your boat. Throw in a good breakfast while you're at it.

*livestrong.com

Something Creative. By creative I don't necessarily mean artistic. There's something primal about the human satisfaction in creating things. To bring something into existence that wouldn't be there without you investing into it. That doesn't have to be 'art'. Carpentry, computer programming, car restoration, magic tricks, or an online business are just a few ideas. There are hundreds of things out there and at least one of them you'll enjoy. This is actually the time I spent writing this book.

In Mason Currey's book "Daily Rituals", he studies the habits of some of history's greatest minds and found that 70% of them did their work first thing in the morning. It's much easier to utilize brainpower for whatever projects you want to pursue without the weight of the day's activities on your mind.

Something Quiet. Think of it as the personal quiet time you don't get enough of. If you're like me, then it's hard making time to sit down and chill out (that's why I became a fan of audiobooks!). Do something quiet you don't often have time for. Meditate, read a good book, actually enjoy that cup of coffee.

You may not have time to do something in all three categories, and that's fine. As always, use what works for you.

Here's what a typical morning looks like for me:

5:00am-5:20am – Morning Routine

5:30am – Leave for gym

5:45am-6:30am – Exercise

7:00am – Breakfast/Read something

7:30am – Write

8:30am – Get dressed and leave for work

Lastly, make sure to reward yourself somehow when completing your morning's activities. Once I finish writing I like to top my mornings off with a few rounds of Words With Friends.

Conclusion

This book has been talking about waking up in the morning, but what it's really about is your life and being proud of how you live it.

I was reading a book one day* and a single sentence struck me: "A person's actions are 100% aligned with how something occurs for him." In other words, our actions are always consistent with our perspective in a given situation.

*The Three Laws of Performance by Steve Zaffron & David Logan

Take for example, guests at a social event. There are those who thrive social settings, while others hyperventilate their way through the evening. There are a lot of reasons why a person would react differently in the same situation, but it all boils down to how the individual experiences the situation. Does going to a party occur to them as something fun, a chance to meet new people and make new friends? Or do they feel threatened being in a place full of people they don't know?

That one sentence shed light on many areas of my life, one of them being my relationship with the alarm clock. I got that I wasn't in control of how I was living my life; I was making decisions according to other people's agendas.

I had to be in school by a certain time, I had to be in work by a certain time. These in turn decided what time I'd wake up day to day.

It suddenly made sense to me. I was sleeping in on weekends and was so lazy during vacation time because waking up occurred to me as something I did for other people. When I didn't "have" to do anything I justified being lazy and loafing around, but the reality is I was getting older just as fast as when I "had" to work. That shift in understanding gave me the resolution to be the decision maker in how my time was spent, which lead to being the decision maker in regards to what time I got up in the morning.

So that poses the question: How does waking up occur for you? Only you'll be able to answer that question fully, but a few common answers are:

- Hard
- Tiring
- A chore
- Something you just have to do

How do you suppose it got like that?

Everything in this book is an actionable step to helping you love waking up, but if there was one thing to remarkably transform how you get up in the morning it would be getting clear on why it is you wake up everyday.

These processes are useful for anyone on any schedule. My hope for you is that, whatever your schedule may be, you find something useful here you can use as a tool to gain control of your life and the direction you're going in.

And remember, waking up earlier isn't just about becoming more efficient and getting more things done in the day. Those are byproducts. It's about living a great life. Don't focus on becoming a machine. Part of what makes a great life is being there for life's moments. Three weeks ago my wife was leaving for South Korea. I woke up to start my day and got through my 20 minute routine when it hit me that my wife was going to be gone for several months. I decided to snuggle up next to her for the next hour before she had to get up and leave for the airport. It's been almost a month now and that memory is still a fond one for me.

With that said, as the original self-made man, Benjamin Franklin, so aptly put:

"*Early to bed and early to rise makes a man healthy, wealthy, and wise*".

To your success.

Recap

Step 1: Waking Up

Cue: _____

Action: _____

Reward: _____

Step 2: Morning Routine

Cue: _____

Action: _____

Reward: _____

Step 3: Evening Routine

Cue: _____

Action: _____

Reward: _____

Completing Your Morning

Something Healthy

Something Creative

Something Quiet

Links

• **Daily Planner**

• **"Power of Habit" Clip**

Can be found at:

www.samuyama.com/love-waking-up

Apps

Wunderlist, Six Wunderkinder

Sleep Cycle, Northcube AB

Other Resources

HabitRPG, OCDevil

This is a great app to help you set good habits. You fight monsters, get gold, and level up by completing tasks and daily habits you set for yourself. You can create a party and go on adventures so a fun thing to do with friends.

SpinMe, Abdulla Al-Shurafa

Another great app for people who have a hard time staying out of bed. It has no snooze, and the only way to turn it off is to stand up and put your thumbprints on it while spinning around in circles.

MyMorningRoutine.com

A collection of interviews with people in a wide variety of fields sharing about how they spend their mornings. Founders of startups and college sport trainers to freelance photographers and world travelers, learn about the morning habits of successful people in a wide range of fields. An incredible resource for ideas and inspiration on how to spend the early hours of the day.

Sam's Insider Mailing List

If you'd like to be the first to hear about upcoming books or get access to other useful productivity tools feel free to email me at me@samuyama.com to be added to my mailing list.

Thank you

Before you go, I'd like to say "thank you" for purchasing my book.

You could have picked from dozens of other books but you took a chance and trusted me to provide something valuable for you.

So from the bottom of my heart, thank you for purchasing this book and reading to the end.

If you like what you read then I need your help! **Please take a moment to leave a review for this book on Amazon.**

This will help me reach others who struggle in the morning and are looking for help, as well as allow me to continue writing books that make a difference in your life. But more than anything, **if you loved what you read then it'll mean the world to me to hear about it :)**

Lastly, I want to follow through on my promise that you get something valuable from this book. If you have any questions, need clarifying on a specific point, or want to get in touch for whatever reason, feel free to email me at me@samuyama.com

Special thanks to Alan, Benjy, Dan, Glenn, &
Zeke for all your help.

Made in the USA
Middletown, DE
25 March 2017